IMAGES
of America

TACOMA
NARROWS BRIDGE

The story of the Tacoma Narrows Bridge is really a three-part series covering the three bridges that have been built so far. The photograph on the cover of this book shows the original bridge, which opened to traffic on July 1, 1940. Pictured here are the 1950 bridge and the 2007 bridge as they appear today. A future bridge, only in the conceptual stage at this time, will include another level below the 2007 bridge for a light-rail link or another roadbed. The towers were designed with sufficient strength to handle the extra load. (Courtesy Mariano Mantel.)

ON THE COVER: On June 28, 1940, these proud construction workers pose in front of the first Tacoma Narrows Bridge just three days before the grand opening on July 1, 1940. They were mostly cement workers who did the last phase of construction. This photograph was taken by Richards Studio of Tacoma. (Courtesy Tacoma Public Library.)

IMAGES
of America

TACOMA
NARROWS BRIDGE

Donald R. Tjossem

ARCADIA
PUBLISHING

Published by Arcadia Publishing
Charleston, South Carolina

Printed in the United States of America

Library of Congress Control Number: 2020946132

For all general information, please contact Arcadia Publishing:
Telephone 843-853-2070
Fax 843-853-0044
E-mail sales@arcadiapublishing.com
For customer service and orders:
Toll-Free 1-888-313-2665

Visit us on the Internet at www.arcadiapublishing.com

To the early Tacoma photographers, without whose efforts and pioneering work this book would not have been possible. Their photographs are held by the Tacoma Public Library and are available for public viewing. The staff of the Northwest Room has always been helpful to inquiries from the public and this author during research. To these people, this publication is dedicated.

This book is also dedicated to all the individuals who worked on the three Tacoma Narrows Bridges. This work requires skill in various technical specialties and can be quite dangerous, as evidenced by some of the photographs in this book.

CONTENTS

ACKNOWLEDGMENTS

I would like to acknowledge the Northwest Room of the Tacoma Public Library for opening its digital files for public download and use in a publication such as this. Especially I would like to thank Brian Kamens and Ilona Perry of the Northwest Room for their help in this project.

Thomas Gotchy was very generous with his assistance and permission to use his grandfather's (Joe Gotchy) photographs for this book. My wife, Becky Alexander, also deserves special mention as she reviewed my writings and made them a lot better than my rough draft. Erin Vosgien, Caroline Anderson, and Jim Kempert, editors at Arcadia Publishing, have been of great help in guiding me from the conception of this book to its final publication. It would not have happened without them.

Unless otherwise noted, all images are from the Tacoma Public Library.

INTRODUCTION

John G. Shindler, a local rancher, is credited with saying to a steamboat captain as they were passing through the Tacoma Narrows, "Captain, some day you will see a bridge over these Narrows." This is reported to have happened in 1888 or 1889. About that time, the Northern Pacific Railroad was considering a trestle, rather than a bridge, across the Narrows between Tacoma and Port Orchard. This was in the early years of the Puget Sound Naval Shipyard, but since it was economically unfeasible at that time, the idea was dropped until nearly 30 years later, when automobiles were in use by most residents of the area.

Eventually, as immigrants came to the New World, new methods were sought to navigate the Salish Sea, as it was called by the early inhabitants who had lived in the area for centuries. One of these options became bridging parts of what is now called Puget Sound with highways. Many islands were bridged early on with short spans, dating to at least 1911. The first and most famous bridge built across the Narrows was arguably "Galloping Gertie," as it was popularly named prior to its collapse on November 7, 1940.

One of the first organized promoters of a Narrows bridge was the Federated Improvement Clubs of Tacoma in 1923. Its campaign for the bridge proposed a span between Point Defiance and the Gig Harbor area. In 1923, the president of the Federated Improvement Clubs told newspaper reporters that the group had been working on the project for a few months.

In 1926, the Tacoma Chamber of Commerce began a campaign endorsing a bridge across the Narrows. The superintendent of Tacoma City Utilities and president of the local Good Roads Association, Llewellyn Evans, spearheaded this early effort.

In 1926, Mitchell Skansie of Gig Harbor was granted a 10-year contract to operate a ferry service between Point Defiance and Gig Harbor. Since this was a 10-year contract, plans were already being made for a crossing when it expired. In 1927, the Roads Committee of the Tacoma Chamber of Commerce determined that a bridge over the Narrows would cost between $3 million and $10 million. This would translate to between $55 million and $185 million in 2020 dollars.

The Washington state legislature passed a law authorizing a Tacoma Narrows Bridge in 1929, and proposals from bridge builders were sent to the county for review. David B. Steinman proposed the first design, which received little support and was eventually dropped due to lack of interest. He would later design the Mackinac Bridge in Michigan, in addition to many other bridges around the world.

Tacoma city engineers came up with a design in 1931 that would carry both automobile and railroad traffic. The estimated cost of $12 million made this plan unrealistic.

In 1932, E.M. Chandler of Olympia proposed to the Tacoma Chamber of Commerce a $3 million suspension bridge. Funding for this proposal was to come from the federal Reconstruction Finance Corporation (RFC). This plan was rejected by the RFC because it was anticipated that not enough cars would use it and pay tolls to pay off the bonds. It would have also cost too much to pay off the no-compete clause in Mitchell Skansie's ferry contract.

During the Great Depression in the 1930s, it was hard to have a serious discussion about funding a bridge of this magnitude. It was not until 1937 that the Washington Toll Bridge Authority (WTBA) was formed by the state legislature that any real progress was made in discussions that would eventually end up with bridge financing.

The WTBA eventually agreed on June 27, 1938, that an RFC loan of $3.3 million and a Public Works Administration (PWA) grant of $2.7 million would finance the bridge. On November 23, 1938, ground breaking was done for the first bridge, and it was completed on July 1, 1940.

The Tacoma Narrows Bridge collapsed on November 7, 1940, due to the engineering and winds of approximately 40 miles per hour, although such winds were not extraordinary for the season or location.

Rebuilding the bridge after the collapse in 1940 was an immediate consideration among the locals and the engineering community. Before serious plans could be made, though, World War II was in full swing, and funding was not a priority. After the war ended in 1945, plans were started again with more support from funding sources.

It was not until Pierce County was able to contribute $1.5 million to guarantee bonds that progress was made on financing the second bridge. When the cost estimate came in for just under $14 million, the WTBA offered a bond issue of $14 million, to be repaid from toll revenues. On March 12, 1948, the financing was completed, and on March 31, the WTBA awarded the contract to build the second bridge to Bethlehem Pacific Coast Steel Corporation and John A. Roebling's Sons of San Francisco. On April 9, 1948, construction began on the second bridge, and it was completed on October 14, 1950.

As time passed and the population increased on both sides of the bridge, it became apparent that consideration should be made for building another bridge across the Narrows. By 2000, the Tacoma Narrows Bridge was carrying 32 million cars and trucks across the water every year. Commuting times between the Kitsap Peninsula and the Tacoma area were unacceptable for traffic going either way, and traffic accidents and fatalities were increasing at an alarming rate.

In 1980, the daily average of vehicles crossing the bridge was 38,973. By 1990, it was 66,573, and by 2000, it was up to 88,000 crossings a day. Something had to be done.

There was some local resistance to building another bridge, as many people did not want the additional development it would bring to the Gig Harbor area. On the other hand, there were residents who wanted the new development on the west side. Eventually, a $615 million contract was signed with Peter Kiewit Sons Inc. and the Bechtel Corporation to build the third bridge and upgrade the existing second one. The ground-breaking ceremony was held on October 5, 2002, and the bridge was opened on July 15, 2007.

One

BEFORE THE BRIDGE(S)

STATE OF WASHINGTON VIEWS.

Rutter, Photo.

Tacoma, Wash.

Native American longboats like these were the primary means of transportation around the Salish Sea (Puget Sound) before the advent of the Mosquito Fleet and before major bridges were built. They were handmade from forest products.

Men in derby hats and suits stand among Native American–style longboats at a shoreside settlement.

Native Americans are pictured close to shore, using their boat to transport goods. In the background is a Northern Pacific Railroad bridge that long preceded the Tacoma Narrows Bridge. This photograph was taken just before the turn of the 20th century.

The steamship *Atalanta* served the Tacoma–Gig Harbor route, as pictured here in 1914. She was the last passenger steamer that ran from Tacoma to Gig Harbor. Later, she was converted to a ferry, and cars were hoisted onto the deck rather than driven on, as is common now.

This photograph was taken by Richards Studio in July 1938 showing where the Tacoma Narrows Bridge would cross. On the left, or west side, with the Bonneville electrical transmission lines visible, is Gig Harbor. To the right is Tacoma, with Point Defiance Park in the background between the two.

If a person were to travel by automobile from Tacoma to Longbranch in 1923, the route would be by leaving Steilacoom on the ferry *Elk*, possibly stopping at Anderson Island, then McNeil Island, and finally docking at the present Longbranch Marina dock. This ferry, built by the Skansie Shipbuilding Company of Gig Harbor, was 67 feet long and held 16 cars. There are no ferries to Longbranch these days, but the trip from Longbranch to Steilacoom only takes one hour by crossing the Narrows Bridge.

This Fairbanks Morse engine was to be placed in the ferryboat *Defiance*, which was under construction. The 360-horsepower engine would propel the ferry at a speed of 10 knots. The men pictured were employees of the Skansie Shipbuilding Company, and they were on the dock in Tacoma for the arrival of this engine.

On January 16, 1927, the Skansie Shipbuilding Company launched the *Defiance*, a new ferry to run on the Washington Navigation Company's route between Gig Harbor and Point Defiance across the Tacoma Narrows. This ferry was 180 feet long and had a capacity of 80 cars. After the 1950 bridge was completed, Olympic Ferries Inc., which operated a ferry route between Port Townsend and Keystone, purchased the *Defiance*. It was eventually converted into a dogfish processor and is no longer in service.

On June 30, 1940, a few days before the opening of the first Narrows Bridge, these Young Men's Business Club (YMBC) members were selling tickets for the last ferry at the Water Carnival at Point Defiance. The ferry *Kalakala* was planning to have a special last cruise on July 2, 1940. Approximately 1,400 tickets were sold, which included dance music by Louis Nomellini's orchestra.

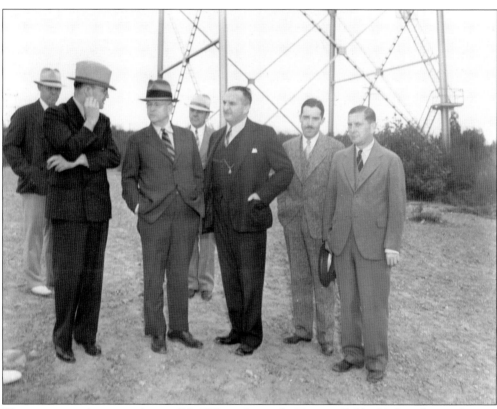

These men are shown on August 26, 1938, in front of a Tacoma Public Utility electrical tower possibly discussing matters pertaining to the building of the Narrows Bridge. From left to right are (first row) Thad Stevenson, secretary/manager of the Tacoma Chamber of Commerce; Harold L. Ickes, secretary of the interior under Roosevelt and Truman; Congressman John M. Coffee; Lacey V. Murrow, state director of highways; and Harold Allen, past president of the Tacoma Chamber of Commerce; (second row) unidentified and M.J. McCaslin of the YMBC.

On July 1, 1940, opening day for the bridge, presidential elections were in full swing. This automobile was decorated with a photograph of Pres. Franklin D. Roosevelt with slogans that read, "He gave us the bridge" and "Watch the Peninsula grow."

Before the first bridge was built, commuters used a ferry to travel from Gig Harbor to Tacoma. This photograph shows the stools passengers could sit on to order a hamburger or hotdog for 10¢; ham sandwiches were 15¢. This counter was aboard the *Skansonia*, which was built by the Skansie Shipbuilding Company in 1929. *Skansonia* was in service until 1967 on other ferry routes. She then came into private hands, and in the mid-1980s, was renovated as a wedding and event venue on Lake Union in Seattle.

The ferryboat *Relief* was used to replace other ferries in the Tacoma area that were in for repairs or maintenance. *Relief* was a 72-foot ferry with an 85-horsepower diesel engine and a 32-foot beam. This was a smaller boat that was only used temporarily and did not carry as many vehicles as the normal ferries.

The ferryboat *Gig Harbor* is shown in Tacoma while the upper deck is being constructed at the Western Boat building on the Wapato Waterway, next to the Western Lumber Manufacturing Company. This photograph was taken on April 16, 1925, only six days after it was launched. The *Gig Harbor* was built originally as a 30-car craft and could be lengthened to 50 cars, if necessary, in the future.

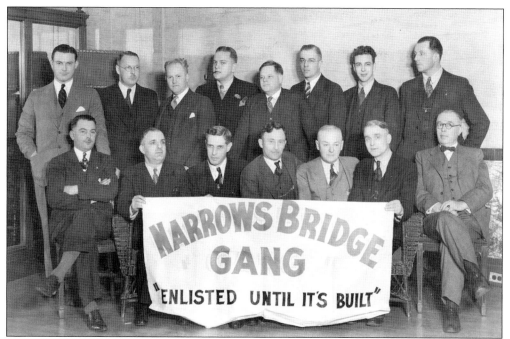

Starting in January 1936, a group called the Narrows Bridge Gang was organized by bridge supporters, a combination of businessmen, community members, and politicians. This group met once a week until November 30, 1938, when contracts were awarded and it was certain that the bridge would be built.

On May 23, 1927, this photograph was taken of the Steilacoom-Longbranch ferry *City of Steilacoom*. There is no ferry service to Longbranch now, but service from Steilacoom continues to McNeil Island, Anderson Island, and Ketron Island.

Much of the equipment and materials used to construct the first bridge were brought in from Titlow Beach, to the immediate south of the construction area. This photograph taken in April 1939 shows the Pacific General Columbia Company dock, which angles off to the right, where much of the material was shipped from. Note the uniformed security officer on the dock.

This photograph was taken in 1939 and artistically modified to show the placement of the Narrows Bridge with a ship painted in. Mount Rainier and Tacoma are at the top, and Gig Harbor and Fox Island are in the lower half.

This event on June 30, 1938, celebrated the award of the $2.7 million PWA grant to build the bridge. Shown are US senator Homer T. Bone at left and Maj. Gen. Walter C. Sweeney, the commanding officer of Fort Lewis, now known as Joint Base Lewis McChord. Much of the work to obtain this grant was done by Senator Bone.

The passenger steamer *Florence K* is docked at the West Side Grocery (now the Tides Tavern) in Gig Harbor. *Florence K* was built in Tacoma in 1903 by Crawford & Reid. At right in this undated photograph is the Skansie Shipbuilding Company. In 1924, *Florence K* was reconstructed as a ferry that could carry 18 vehicles. She was later named *Gloria* and finally *Beeline* before being scrapped sometime after 1945.

There were many festivities, luncheons, and dinners in the area to commemorate the opening of the bridge. This edible Narrows Bridge was served at the home of Elizabeth H. Walton on July 1, 1940. Large pieces of cake make up the bulk of the bridge, while deviled egg boats float around and under the bridge on a gelatin sea. Stalks of broccoli and celery make up the greenery.

This view is looking west toward Gig Harbor after the construction of the towers for the first bridge had been completed. Both towers were completed by November 1939. Yet to be completed are the main suspension cables, the suspenders, and the roadway. What appear to be suspension cables are actually the catwalks that would be used for access to the main cables as they were put in place.

These steelworkers from the Structural Iron Workers Union Local 114 are in a parade on the way to the celebration at the Stadium Bowl for the PWA grant to begin construction on the Narrows Bridge. The event was on June 30, 1938.

This is an artist's rendition of what the bridge would look like after completion. The sketch depicts an aerial view from Tacoma facing west toward Gig Harbor and the Olympic Peninsula. This is an early conceptual map of the Narrows Bridge, as Highway 16 does not yet exist and there is basically no development in the Gig Harbor area. The Purdy Bridge is visible at upper right. This map would have been shown during early promotions of the bridge.

This was the headquarters for the State of Washington Engineers, headed by Clark Eldridge, in 1939. The building was about a mile from the construction site. Before supervising the construction of the Narrows Bridge, Eldridge worked on the first Lake Washington floating bridge. These state-employed engineers worked as a team with the private engineers and design consultants who were hired by the state.

This is the interior of the engineering headquarters for the construction of the first Narrows Bridge. Note the formal attire of the engineers and close working quarters. The design consultants were Leon Moisseiff for the superstructure and Moran & Proctor of New York for the substructure.

This 1939 aerial view shows where all the cement came from for the construction of the first Narrows Bridge. This cement plant was on the west side of the bridge landing, where Gig Harbor is now.

This is the mixing dock built to mix cement for the construction of the first Narrows Bridge. All the concrete for the west anchorage was made at this plant, which has long been demolished, as it was no longer necessary.

Cement anchor piers were dumped into Puget Sound after being hauled to the proper location at the bridge site. These concrete anchors were 12 by 12 by 51 ½ feet. Each weighed 550 tons and they were manufactured at the Scofield plant in Tacoma. The anchors were to hold caissons in place against the swift currents of the Narrows. Thirty-two anchors were used for the east pier, and 24 were used for the west pier caissons. A total of 103,129 cubic yards of concrete were used.

A caisson forms the base of the piers that support the towers of the bridge. These huge structures were built of concrete sheathed in wood and had a steel cutting edge on the bottom for digging into the silt on the floor of the Narrows. The caisson was the bottom section of the pier, and sections were added to the top of it. The derricks were used for lifting as the caisson sank.

Diver Johnny Bacon is shown in his diving suit with attendees before making a 90-foot dive into the Narrows to place a cable around a broken anchor block. Bacon is wearing his 200-pound diving suit; below, a 45-pound helmet is being placed on his head. Dives into the Narrows were normally limited to 15–45 minutes during slack tide because the currents were so swift otherwise. These images were taken on May 12, 1939.

This is an early stage of bridge construction after the towers were put into place in 1939. The catwalks are in place for working on the main suspension cable, while none of the roadway has yet been built. (Courtesy Washington State Department of Transportation.)

These 11 construction workers are working on the early stages of the first Narrows Bridge. All are wearing hard hats, and a few have their tools hanging from their waists. Note the pile of rebar on the left and lumber on the right. The roadbed of the bridge has not yet been completed and can be seen hanging behind their heads. Both completed towers are seen in the background. The average number of workers on the bridge most of the time was about 200. As the bridge neared completion, the number nearly doubled. Most employees worked an eight-hour shift and put in a 40-hour week. (Courtesy Washington State Historical Society.)

What was advertised as the last ferry ride across the Narrows took place on July 2, 1940. About 1,440 passengers bought tickets and boarded at the Tacoma Municipal Dock (pictured) and at Point Defiance for the ride to Gig Harbor. The streamlined *Kalakala* was in service at that time. *Kalakala* was listed in the National Register of Historic Places on March 22, 2006, and was scrapped in January 2015.

These members of the YMBC Narrows Bridge Committee donned festive hats on June 30, 1940, the day before the bridge's grand opening, while they prepared for the 1940 Water Carnival at Point Defiance. This organization sponsored the last ferry ride from Tacoma aboard the *Kalakala*.

These passengers on the *Kalakala* are dressed in early-20th-century costumes for a dance on the last ferry from Tacoma. Of course, this did not turn out to be the last ferry ride, as the Tacoma Narrows Bridge would collapse after being open just four months, and the ferries would be put back into service for another 10 years until the second Tacoma Narrows Bridge could be built.

On June 30, 1938, a celebration was held at the Stadium Bowl for the Works Progress Administration grant to build the Narrows Bridge. The five men sitting in the first row are Tacoma mayor Dr. John Siegle, Washington governor Clarence Martin, commanding officer at Fort Lewis Maj. Gen. Walter C. Sweeney, US senator Homer T. Bone, and F. Rodman Titcomb of the Tacoma Chamber of Commerce.

Appearing on a special campaign train in Tacoma are, from left to right, Arthur B. Langlie, Republican candidate for governor; Edith Willkie; Wendell Willkie, a Republican presidential candidate; Paul Preus, candidate for Congress; and unidentified. Langlie was mayor of Seattle on this date, September 23, 1940, only 115 days after the Narrows Bridge was opened and 45 days before it collapsed.

Spectators await the opening ceremonies on the west side of the Narrows Bridge on July 1, 1940. Prior to the opening of the bridge, a band from the Puget Sound Naval Station entertained thousands on the west side, while a band from the 10th Field Artillery from Fort Lewis entertained on the east side.

For the west side opening of the first Narrows Bridge, Adm. Edward B. Fenner is shown cutting the ribbon. To his immediate right is Homer Jones, the mayor of Bremerton. There was no representation from Gig Harbor, which was not yet an incorporated city.

Pictured about to cut the ribbon for the east side ribbon-cutting ceremonies are, from left to right, state highway director Lacey V. Morrow (holding hat), Ralph Keenan of Pacific Bridge Company, Maj. A.P. Kitson, Col. Kenneth S. Perkins (cutting ribbon), Capt. R.S. McClenaghan, consulting engineer C.E. Andrews, Gov. Clarence D. Martin, and celebration chairman Ted Brown. The west end was opened by the US Navy and the east end was opened by the US Army, which have major installations on their respective sides of the bridge.

On July 1, 1940, this 1923 Lincoln touring car was the first automobile to cross the Tacoma Narrows Bridge and pay a toll. Governor Martin is seated at front center. This vehicle had carried both Queen Elizabeth II and President Roosevelt for other events at different venues. It is presently on display at America's Car Museum in Tacoma.

On opening day, this entourage passed through the toll gates from the east, heading toward Gig Harbor for the first-ever tolled crossing of the Narrows Bridge. There was another dedication ceremony on the Gig Harbor side, and then the entourage returned to Tacoma.

Two

THE FIRST BRIDGE

This is probably the most iconic photograph of the Tacoma Narrows Bridge collapse. It was taken by James Bashford at 11:00 a.m. on November 7, 1940. From 1939 to mid-1940, Bashford worked for Thompson Photo Service and took over 400 photographs of the bridge's construction. He passed away in Tacoma on July 3, 1949, at the age of 72. (Courtesy Library of Congress.)

Adm. Daniel E. Barbey is cutting the ribbon at the grand opening of the first Narrows Bridge on the Gig Harbor side. He is accompanied by, from left to right, Adm. H.E. Haven, commander of the Navy yard; Capt. H.B. Butterfield, commander of the Tacoma group of the reserve fleet; Comdr. C.A. Berry of the Tacoma Naval Station; Comdr. Franklin K. Zinn, inspector of the Tacoma Naval Reserve; and Lt. Comdr. J.W. Philippbar. A large contingent of Navy sailors and an honor guard are standing at attention. The automobiles in the background are anxiously waiting to become some of the first vehicles to cross the new bridge.

Gov. Clarence D. Martin is shown receiving change from a toll taker on the very first toll collected on opening day, July 1, 1940. The toll was 55¢ for the car and driver plus 15¢ for each passenger. Norton Clapp, developer and industrialist, is in the front seat. Tacoma mayor Harry P. Cain and his wife, Marjorie, are in the back.

This west-facing view on July 1, 1940, shows the first vehicle to cross the Narrows Bridge with Governor Martin and Mayor Cain. On this first day, 2,053 cars crossed the bridge. A normal day in 2020 would see approximately 42,000 westbound cars and 28,000 eastbound cars crossing the two current bridges. The disparity in the numbers is because tolls are only charged going east, and many drivers plan their trips accordingly.

On August 29, 1940, this is what the toll lanes looked like facing west from the Tacoma side of the bridge. Tolls were only charged traveling from the east side to the west side. It was assumed that this one-way fee would cover the return trip as well, but some frugal individuals would drive around from Gig Harbor or the Kitsap Peninsula to Olympia and back to Tacoma to avoid the fare.

Engineers had been concerned about oscillations of the Narrows Bridge even while it was being constructed in February 1939. The WTBA and the PWA hired engineering professor F. Burt Farquharson of the University of Washington to study the bridge's wave motions. When the bridge swayed gently, as seen here, people would drive across for entertainment. The whitecaps on the water below attest to the wind speeds when this photograph was taken.

The bridge was nicknamed "Galloping Gertie" even before it was completed because it would sway on windy days. The bridge would at times be shut down due to high winds, if it was determined it was unsafe to cross. This is a view from the roadbed on the day it collapsed, when high winds produced stronger oscillations than usual.

Professor Farquharson, there to document the collapse for his studies, was the last man to leave the Narrows Bridge. He was bitten by Tubby on his index finger as he attempted to save the dog. Farquharson was able to get to safety before the bridge fell. The images on these two pages are stills from the movie he was filming. (Courtesy Library of Congress.)

This photograph was taken by Richards Studio of Tacoma at the moment the Tacoma Narrows Bridge broke apart and fell into Puget Sound. Since it was known that something out of the ordinary was happening to the bridge that day, the collapse is well documented in both photographs and motion pictures.

This view from the east side shortly after the collapse of the Narrows Bridge shows how the roadbed sagged. It is quite apparent that the bridge is broken by looking at the crack across the road in the foreground.

Looking west after the collapse, it was apparent that most of the bridge was underwater and only parts of it remained intact. What remains of the bridge, both underwater and above, was listed in the National Register of Historic Places on August 31, 1992. As early as December 1940, a contract was awarded to J.H. Pomeroy & Company for the removal of the remaining superstructure.

This view of the bridge, looking toward the north, shows how parts of it were still attached. This classic scene was photographed for days following the collapse since it took some time for the damage to be surveyed and evaluated. The actual collapse of the bridge lasted approximately one hour, from 10:03 a.m., when traffic was stopped, until 11:10 a.m.

From the southern side of the bridge on the west side, this view shows the shreds of Galloping Gertie hanging into Puget Sound after the collapse. Two men on the right are walking along the railroad tracks to get a closer look. News of the collapse traveled quickly, and thousands of visitors came to see the devastation.

These two men are looking west at what was left of the Narrows Bridge after its collapse. The fact that the bridge was so slender, with only two lanes for traffic, and did not have any stabilizing girders, contributed to its demise. Engineers and contractors were not held accountable for the collapse, although an insurance agent, Hallett R. French, who had pocketed premiums paid by the state, was sentenced to 15 years in prison. He served two years and was released for good behavior.

This is what was left of the bridge as viewed from the Tacoma side, from the approach. Note how the suspenders no longer supported the roadway in a level manner. The design consultants were Leon Moisseiff for the superstructure and Moran & Proctor of New York for the substructure. Clark Eldridge was the Washington state engineer for the layout design.

Frederick Farquharson was a University of Washington professor who worked for Boeing early in his career. He went on to head the university's Engineering Experiment Station and became a world-recognized authority on aerodynamic testing for bridge design. He was hired as a consultant to determine how to stop the bridge's vibration months before the collapse and was on the bridge taking motion pictures of the structure as it failed.

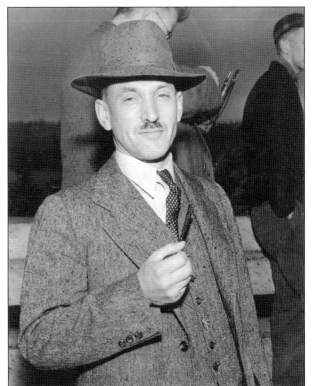

These somber men are, from left to right, Patrick H. Winston, secretary of the WTBA; James A. Davis, acting highway director; Clark H. Eldridge, project engineer; Charles W. Andrew, chief engineer; and Frederick Farquharson, professor at the University of Washington. This photograph was taken on the day the Tacoma Narrows Bridge collapsed, November 7, 1940.

This is a remaining fragment of the collapsed Narrows Bridge. For many years, parts of the bridge were on the beach for anyone who wanted to take one as a souvenir. Now, what remains of the bridge is listed in the National Register of Historic Places and it is illegal to take any of the remains, either on the beach or underwater. The towers and any steel that was salvageable were recovered and used in the World War II effort.

Under the west end of the second Narrows Bridge, the last remaining visible part of the original bridge can be seen: the support structure for the off-ramp from second bridge for westbound traffic. These remains were determined to still be structurally sound enough to be used again for the second bridge. (Author's collection.)

The chairman of the Pierce County Board of Commissioners, Harvey O. Scofield (left), and the auditor and clerk of the board, Joseph E. Ford, are shown signing 1,500 bonds at $1,000 each to guarantee interest payments on the $14 million Tacoma Narrows bridge bond. This photograph was taken on April 12, 1948, very shortly after construction had begun on April 9 for the second bridge.

US vice president Alben Barkley (far left) is being presented a Richards Studio framed photograph of the Tacoma Narrows bridge by members of the Pierce County Democratic Committee in Tacoma on October 11, 1950, a few days before the opening of the second bridge. Congressman John Coffee is at center, holding the photograph, and Sen. Warren G. Magnuson is to the right.

The old Narrows Bridge anchors had to be destroyed to make way for the new ones for the second bridge. This two-ton steel ball was swung from a crane to break up reinforced concrete on the anchors for the original bridge. Dexter R. Smith began the design for the second bridge on July 15, 1941. The contract to dismantle what was left of the bridge was awarded to Philip Murphy & Woodworth Company in August 1942 and was completed in June 1943.

New approaches had to be built for the second bridge. This photograph shows a dynamite explosion used in the early stages of rebuilding the approach on the east side. These dynamite blasts were used in addition to the two-ton steel ball crane shown on the previous page for destruction of the old approaches and anchors.

This view shows the steel roadbed construction just starting from the west side. The suspenders, which will support the roadbed from the main suspension cable, can be seen and are ready to be attached as the steelwork progresses. The catwalks and suspension cables above are also in place.

Steelworkers are closing the gap in the under support for the roadbed of the second bridge. This photograph was taken on May 31, 1950, as the bridge roadbed steelwork was nearing completion.

This view shows the steelwork for the roadbed as it is nearing completion. The railroad bed on the beach can be seen in the background. Construction started on the second bridge on April 9, 1948, and was completed on October 14, 1950.

Reinforced rods are being laid for the roadbed as the bridge is approaching completion. Also shown are exposed plywood deck forms under the steel rebar.

These two photographs taken from the east tower show the differences in development the bridge made to the Tacoma area. The photograph at right was taken in 1940, just prior to the completion of the first bridge. The photograph below was taken from the east tower of the 1950 bridge in 1998 during a survey by the Historic American Engineering Record division of the National Park Service.

Looking east toward Tacoma and Mount Rainier in this view taken on August 2, 1950, the rebar for the roadbed has been laid and is ready for cement. Bethlehem Pacific Coast Steel Corporation did the steelwork for this part of the bridge.

This photograph shows the fearlessness of the steelworkers working on the bridge. Two workers are climbing up this crane's boom. Safety harnesses were not a requirement in the days when this bridge was built. (Joe Gotchy photograph; courtesy Thomas Gotchy.)

The roadbed forms for the bridge were made of lumber and plywood. The Douglas Fir Plywood Association had these photographs taken of workers laying the sheets of plywood.

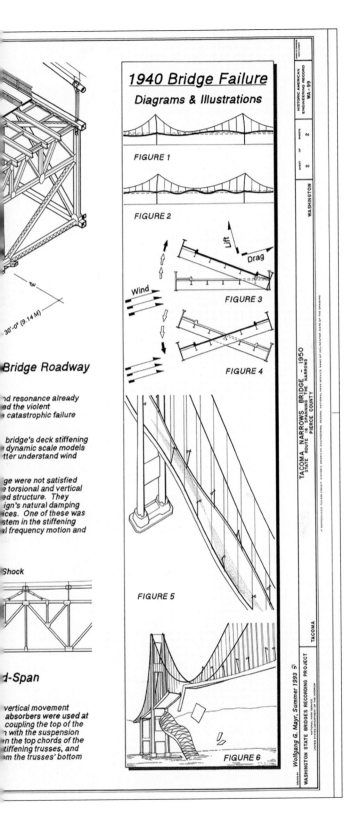

TACOMA NARROWS BRIDGE – 1950
STATE ROUTE 16 SPANNING THE NARROWS
PIERCE COUNTY

HISTORIC AMERICAN ENGINEERING RECORD WA-99

WASHINGTON

SHEET 2 OF 2

Wolfgang G. Mayr, Summer 1993

WASHINGTON STATE BRIDGES RECORDING PROJECT
NATIONAL PARK SERVICE
UNDER UNITED STATES DEPARTMENT OF THE INTERIOR

TACOMA

1940 Bridge Failure
Diagrams & Illustrations

FIGURE 1

FIGURE 2

Lift

Drag

Wind

FIGURE 3

FIGURE 4

FIGURE 5

FIGURE 6

30'-0" (9.14 M)

Bridge Roadway

...nd resonance already
...ed the violent
...e catastrophic failure

...bridge's deck stiffening
...dynamic scale models
...tter understand wind

...ge were not satisfied
...e torsional and vertical
...ed structure. They
...ign's natural damping
...ices. One of these was
...stem in the stiffening
...al frequency motion and

Shock

...d-Span

...vertical movement
...absorbers were used at
...coupling the top of the
...n with the suspension
...n the top chords of the
...tiffening trusses, and
...m the trusses' bottom

These drawings show the differences in tower and roadbed construction of the 1940 and 1950 bridges. The major difference is that the 1940 version was a two-lane bridge and the 1950 version was increased to four lanes. A damping system was also added to increase the stability of the bridge, in addition to strengthening the entire truss system. (Courtesy Library of Congress.)

Looking east toward Tacoma, the steelwork has been finished for the bridge, and it is ready to have the concrete forms and pavement laid for completion of the roadbed.

The catwalks are completed and suspended from the two towers. The suspenders are hanging down, ready to support the roadbed as it is built. When the bridge was completed, there was no hesitation at all for the general public to use it. They had waited for nearly 10 years for it to be built and were tired of riding the ferries.

This photograph shows the second Narrows Bridge half built. To the left is Gig Harbor (the west side); eventually, the construction from Tacoma (the east side) will complete the bridge.

John A. Roebling's Sons company officials are reviewing the cables to be used in the second phase of the bridge construction. Bethlehem Pacific Coast Steel Corporation had completed the towers on July 16, 1949, and the spinning and stringing of the cables was about to begin.

A workman is sitting at the controls of the machinery used for spinning cable from the two large spools of cable. These larger cables were used to make the catwalks that were put into place so that workmen could work on the suspension cables as they were being put in place later.

Steelwork is being placed for the roadbed on the second bridge. This view is facing east toward Tacoma. This and the following photograph were taken in the spring of 1950. Just getting the steel into place made construction of the bridge a major challenge, not to mention the height above the water and any unfavorable weather conditions.

Most of the steelwork has been laid for the roadbed, and cement forms are about to be put in place for laying the concrete and asphalt. Note how undeveloped the east side of the bridge is, even though it is in Tacoma.

On July 27, 1950, men are laying plywood, which was to be part of the roadbed for the new Narrows Bridge. Douglas fir plywood was used a lot more than many people realize in making the forms for the concrete pours on the roadbed. The man in the white shirt with no hard hat at left was most likely the driver of the truck, helping to unload the prefabricated forms, as he is not dressed for working all day on the bridge.

Two men from John A. Roebling's Sons are working with a coil of wire that will be spun into cable for the suspension bridge. Roebling's worked on the next phase of the bridge, after Bethlehem Pacific Coast Steel completed the work on the towers on July 16, 1949.

These are strands of cable that will be used for the suspension cables after the spinning process takes place. The hoisting equipment used to move these bales of wire is in the background.

This photograph shows the second bridge as it appeared upon completion in the fall of 1950. The undeveloped area of Gig Harbor is seen at left before it became a city, and Point Defiance Park is above the bridge. This view is looking north, with Vashon Island beyond Point Defiance. (Courtesy Washington State Department of Transportation.)

These men are standing on a catwalk, which enables them to work on the main suspension cable for the roadway, which is 20.25 inches in diameter. There are 8,705 strands of No. 6 wire in each of the two cables that suspend the roadway. (Joe Gotchy photograph; courtesy Thomas Gotchy.)

Gov. Arthur B. Langlie is shown giving a speech to open the second Tacoma Narrows Bridge on October 14, 1950. He praised the construction of the new bridge, which showed "a faith and courage typical of that of the American people." This second bridge was an $18 million project, of which $4 million was paid to the State of Washington as a settlement for Galloping Gertie.

Woody Wood (left) and Hank Meir (right) are replacing pins with bolts 200 feet above the Narrows. Suspender cables, not yet attached, can be seen at left. The catwalks for working on the main suspension cable can be seen above. (Joe Gotchy photograph; courtesy Thomas Gotchy.)

This is a close-up and detailed view of the eastern (Tacoma side) tower. This tower reached to a height of 507 feet above the water (mean sea level). The height above the piers is 467 feet, and above the roadway the height was 307 feet. (Courtesy Library of Congress.)

George Scofield Company did a lot of the cement work on the Narrows Bridge. The company's office was at 1543 Dock Street and J. Elmer Alskog was president of the business. For the second bridge, 50,000 cubic yards of concrete were used just for the two anchorages.

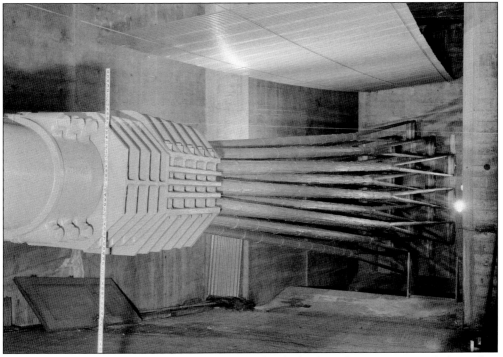

This is a view of the southeast cable anchorage under the bridge. The measuring stick shows that it is approximately three feet off the ground and three feet thick.

This photograph was taken from the east tower, facing west toward Gig Harbor in 1993. Wolfgang Mayr, a summer intern for the International Council on Monuments and Sites, is standing on the suspension cable at right. (Courtesy Library of Congress.)

This photograph, facing west, shows Wolfgang Mayr, who was a delineator for the Historic American Engineering Record. He contributed to the drawings shown on pages 60–61 and 76–77 comparing the first and second Narrows Bridges. (Courtesy Library of Congress.)

This photograph shows spectators enjoying the opening day of the second bridge on October 14, 1950. The toll on that opening day was 55¢ for a car and 15¢ for a pedestrian. People were delighted to pay these tolls to participate in the opening day event. The walkway on the second bridge is now blocked off to pedestrians, but there is a wider and safer walkway on the newer third bridge.

This photograph, taken in 1993 at the center of the second bridge, shows the anti-sway bracing attached to the main suspension cable, a design improvement to combat the problem the first bridge had. Obvious improvements to this bridge include a wider roadbed of four lanes, and grating that can be seen between the car lanes to let air pass through. (Courtesy Library of Congress.)

This view of the eastern tower was taken in 1993 and shows the distinctive design of the towers used in the 1950s-era construction. Following the collapse of the original bridge, this design earned the structure the name of "Sturdy Gertie." (Courtesy Library of Congress.)

This photograph was taken looking toward Tacoma and shows the main suspension cable heading up to the eastern tower. Note the handrails on the suspension cable used by maintenance workers for access all the way to the top of the tower.

Four

THE THIRD BRIDGE

On opening day of the third bridge on July 7, 2007, thousands of walkers, runners, and others can be seen on the newest span before it opened to traffic. Everyone was celebrating the long-awaited opening of the third bridge. This photograph is facing west toward Gig Harbor, and cars can still be seen on the older span used for two-way traffic until the newest bridge opened. The additional bridge was necessary to accommodate the commuter traffic to and from Gig Harbor and Tacoma. This bridge cut the driving time from McChord Air Base to Bremerton Naval shipyard in half, from 1 hour 45 minutes to 55 minutes at a speed of 45 miles per hour, or from 79 miles to 39 miles.

These steel decks are the first of three loads being brought in to construct the third bridge. The steel came from Japan, and they were fabricated in South Korea. The decks had just completed a 5,250-mile trip across the Pacific Ocean that took 18 days.

This photograph shows where the suspension cable enters the anchorage for the bridge. There are four of these, one on each side of the road and at each end. Each concrete anchorage, most of which is underground, weighs 81 million pounds. (Author's collection.)

This interesting view shows the contrast in construction between the 1950 (left) and 2007 bridges. Advances in technology and engineering skill account for the differences that can be seen here. (Courtesy Nick Mealey.)

These six toll booths are ready to take fares from traffic crossing the present Narrows Bridge. The lines are quite long sometimes, even though electronic payment is possible as well as payment by mail. The 2019 fiscal year toll revenues were $82.25 million. (Author's collection.)

This toll taker is in the process of accepting payment. Tolls are only taken on vehicles heading east into Tacoma, so essentially all tolls collected are for a round trip. It is anticipated that tolls will no longer need to be collected after 2031, if traffic counts remain at the present level. (Author's collection.)

This is a close-up of the original Tacoma Narrows Bridge support beam, which is part of the National Historical Site designation, on the west end of the bridge. This part of the original bridge was determined salvageable and is still in use today on the 1950 bridge. (Courtesy Chris Sawtelle.)

To this day, drivers are reminded that there may be severe side winds as they cross the Narrows Bridge. There have not been any winds strong enough to cause swaying or movement on the last two bridges built that would even begin to compare to the first bridge's disaster. (Author's collection.)

With all the present-day technology of weather reporting and prediction, there is still a windsock to visually show which direction and how strong the winds are by direct observation. Wind has not been a threat to the present two bridges, and no swaying or problems have affected the bridges, even with winds up to 100 miles per hour. The bridge has been closed at times due to falling ice from the towers or from winds that could affect traffic. (Author's collection.)

This view, looking northeast, shows the base of the eastern tower, designated as tower five. This pier penetrated 90 feet into the bottom of Puget Sound in 135 feet of water, and had a total height of 265 feet. (Courtesy Library of Congress.)

This photograph dramatically shows the difference in construction of the towers of the two bridges in use today. The 1950 tower in the background is made of steel, while the 2007 bridge's towers were built using reinforced concrete. Economy and strength drove the decision to use concrete for the newest bridge. (Author's collection.)

These two photographs show the differences in bridge design but also how they complement each other. Above is the 1950 bridge, and below is the 2007 bridge. The construction of the 2007 bridge was done with simpler designs and additional strength due to the changes in engineering and technology. (Author's collection.)

This is an abandoned toll takers' break room. It is hard to imagine how difficult it would have been to be confined to tiny toll booths for most of the day. They certainly deserved every break they were able to take in this small building. There were similar facilities on each side of the bridge, so the toll takers did not have to cross all lanes of traffic to take a break.

While the third bridge was under construction, people crossing the second bridge were able to get a close-up view of what was happening. In this photograph, the catwalks are in place, and the main suspension cable has been installed. The two gantry cranes, which rode on the suspension cables like railroad track, are getting ready to lift the deck section, waiting below on a barge. (Courtesy Neil Sanchala.)

This photograph shows the distinct contrasts in the design of both the towers and roadbed trusses for the second and third bridges. The differences in design are a result of over 50 years of technology, but at the same time, they complement each other. (Courtesy Ryan Stavely.)

The contrast in the two bridge designs is very apparent in this photograph taken facing Gig Harbor. The original part of the first bridge, an approach support, is seen between the two towers. The Bonneville Power tower, supporting lines across the Narrows, is also visible to the right. The newer bridge was designed so that the two beams of the towers were not exactly parallel. This difference in width added strength to the towers. (Courtesy Kevin Madden.)

This is another view of the toll takers' break building that was used for the first and second bridges. It is presently vacant and in disrepair, as it has not been used since tolls were discontinued on the second bridge on May 14, 1965, thirteen years ahead of schedule. Tolls are now paid electronically, by cash, by credit card, or by mail.

This is the entryway to an elevator that takes maintenance crews to the top of the tower on the third bridge. It is not always necessary to walk up the suspension cables. Only authorized maintenance staff can use the elevator unless they are taking a very privileged guest to the top of the tower. (Author's collection.)

This photograph shows the difference in construction of the two towers that were built over five decades apart but maintain design compatibility. It was especially important to the designers of the third bridge that it fit in aesthetically with the community and the second bridge. (Courtesy Washington State Department of Transportation.)

The Narrows Bridges are near residential areas, so consideration had to be made that would suppress traffic noise. Following completion of the bridges, noise was still an issue, but it was eventually addressed and suppressed to the local residents' satisfaction. (Author's collection.)

Boating is year-round recreation in the Tacoma Narrows. This boat is seen through a suspender holding up the bridge roadway. Boaters are wary of the swift currents of the Narrows and understand that the safest time for boating is during an ebb tide. (Author's collection.)

The opening of the third Tacoma Narrows Bridge on July 15, 2007, brought a lot of celebrations, parties, paraphernalia, and ephemera for the event. The opportunity was given for runners and walkers to enjoy crossing the bridge before it was opened to traffic, and thousands took advantage. Shown above is the participant T-shirt for the bridge run, and below is a medal that the Harbor History Museum issued for the event. (Both, author's collection.)

Becky Alexander is reflected on the granite monument at the War Memorial Park on the Tacoma side of the bridge. The historical markers and monuments were placed by the Tacoma Historical Society, which holds an annual memorial service at the park. (Author's collection.)

This classic photograph shows both bridges with Mount Rainier in the background. It was taken from the west side in Gig Harbor. On a day like this, people like to say, "The mountain is out." The weather is not always like this in the Puget Sound area. (Author's collection.)

Don Tjossem and Becky Alexander participated in the opening of the third Narrows Bridge on July 15, 2007. An estimated 6,000 people showed up to take part in the daylong events to commemorate the opening of the long-awaited bridge. (Author's collection.)

BIBLIOGRAPHY

Agricultural and Mechanical College of Texas. *The Failure of the Tacoma Narrows Bridge*. College Station, TX: School of Engineering Texas Engineering Experiment Station, 1944.

Andrew, Charles E. *Final Report on Tacoma Narrows Bridge*. Tacoma, WA: Washington Toll Bridge Authority, 1952.

Carmody, John M. *The Failure of the Tacoma Narrows Bridge*. Washington, DC: United States Federal Works Agency, 1941.

Carson, Rob, and Dean J. Koepfler. *Masters of Suspension: The Men and Women Who Bridged the Tacoma Narrows Once Again*. Tacoma, WA: *Tacoma News Tribune*, 2007.

Goldstone, Bruce. *The Rise and Fall of Galloping Gertie*. New York, NY: McGraw-Hill, 1999.

Gotchy, Joe. *Bridging the Narrows*. Gig Harbor, WA: Peninsula Historical Society, 1990.

Harvey, Paul W. *Tacoma Headlines: An Account of Tacoma News and Newspapers from 1873 to 1962*. Tacoma, WA: *Tacoma News Tribune*, 1962.

Heritage League of Pierce County. *A History of Pierce County Washington 1990*. Dallas, TX: Taylor Publishing Company, 1990.

Hobbs, Richard S. *Catastrophe to Triumph: Bridges of the Tacoma Narrows*. Pullman, WA: Washington State University Press, 2006.

Hunt, Herbert, and Floyd C. Kaylor. *Washington West of the Cascades*. Chicago, IL: S.J. Clarke Publishing Company, 1917.

Jepsen, David J., and David J. Norberg. *Contested Boundaries*. Hoboken, NJ: Wiley Blackwell, 2017.

MacGougan, Denny. *Tacoma*. Fox Island, WA: Baker/Anderson Enterprises, 2003.

Peters, Nick. *Historic Photos of Tacoma*. Nashville, TN: Turner Publishing Company, 2007.

Petroski, Henry. *To Engineer is Human*. New York, NY: Vintage Books, 1992.

Robinson, John V. *Bridging the Tacoma Narrows*. Crockett, CA: Carquinez Press, 2007.

Discover Thousands of Local History Books
Featuring Millions of Vintage Images

Arcadia Publishing, the leading local history publisher in the United States, is committed to making history accessible and meaningful through publishing books that celebrate and preserve the heritage of America's people and places.

Find more books like this at
www.arcadiapublishing.com

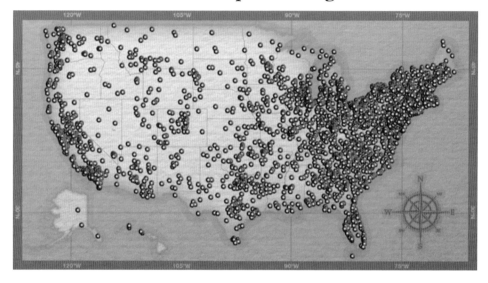

Search for your hometown history, your old stomping grounds, and even your favorite sports team.

Consistent with our mission to preserve history on a local level, this book was printed in South Carolina on American-made paper and manufactured entirely in the United States. Products carrying the accredited Forest Stewardship Council (FSC) label are printed on 100 percent FSC-certified paper.

MADE IN THE USA